Tripp's Ventures GEORGIA

Fueling the Passion to Travel

Written by Michael Perry & Meitra Lak Perry, Ed.S.

Illustrated by Lisa Greenleaf

Copyright © 2019 AMMP Publishing, LLC

{ **Venture** [ven-chər]
verb: Undertake a risky or daring journey or course of action. }

Copyright © 2019 AMMP Publishing, LLC

All rights reserved. This publication may not be reproduced, stored in retrieval system, or transmitted in whole or in part, in any form or by any means, electronic, mechanical, photocopying, recording, or otherwise, without the prior written permission of AMMP Publishing, LLC.

The scanning, uploading or distribution of this book via the Internet or any other means without the express permission of the publisher is illegal and punishable by law. Please purchase only authorized electronic editions of this work and do not participate in or encourage piracy of copyrighted materials, electronically or otherwise.

No responsibility for loss caused to any individual or organization acting on or refraining from action as a result of the material in this publications can be accepted by AMMP Publishing, LLC or the authors.

To order additional copies of this book contact:
AMMP Publishing, LLC
AMMPpublishing@gmail.com

Perry, Meitra Lak; Perry, Michael
Tripp's Ventures: GEORGIA, Fueling the Passion to Travel;
Cover, book design, product development, and illustrations by Lisa Greenleaf

Summary: *Tripp's Ventures: GEORGIA* seeks to spark the desire to travel at a young age by encouraging readers to experience locations unique to the state of Georgia.

ISBN: 978-0-9801171-3-4

This book was printed in the United States of America

Welcome to Tripp's Ventures: GEORGIA. I'm Tripp the Raccoon. In this book, I will share with you some of the most amazing places in the state of Georgia. From Native American beginnings to modern landmarks, we will leave no stone unturned!

Be on the lookout for "Tripp's Tips" throughout this book. There, I will share with you all the magnificent places I have traveled to and hopefully inspire you to see the places for yourself!

The world is waiting for you to discover it, so venture on and see what Georgia has to offer!

ABOUT VENTURE BOOKS:

Traveling is an important part of broadening our perspective and understanding the world around us. It pushes us out of our comfort zones. Travel allows us to experience and understand different cultures which could be just beyond your front door. Venture Book Series is about instilling the desire to travel at a young age. We believe you don't have to travel far from home to find unique landscapes, exciting adventures, and immerse yourself in history. Often there are gems just beyond our backyard, but it is up to us to go find them.

Venture Books highlights geography, history, and experiences which make the locations unique from others. It is also important to visit these places to ensure the preservation of these locations. We hope Venture Books will inspire readers to visit each place and fuel the desire to constantly expand their world perspective.

MAP OF GEORGIA

Draw a star over where you live in the United States.

GEOGRAPHY:

Georgia is a land of contrast. There are ancient mountains with dramatic waterfalls in north Georgia and warm sandy beaches near the coast. There are small charming towns and expansive cities with towering skyscrapers. There are communities that revolve around growing crops and cities which serve as headquarters for some of the largest companies in the world.

Atlanta skyline, the capital of Georgia

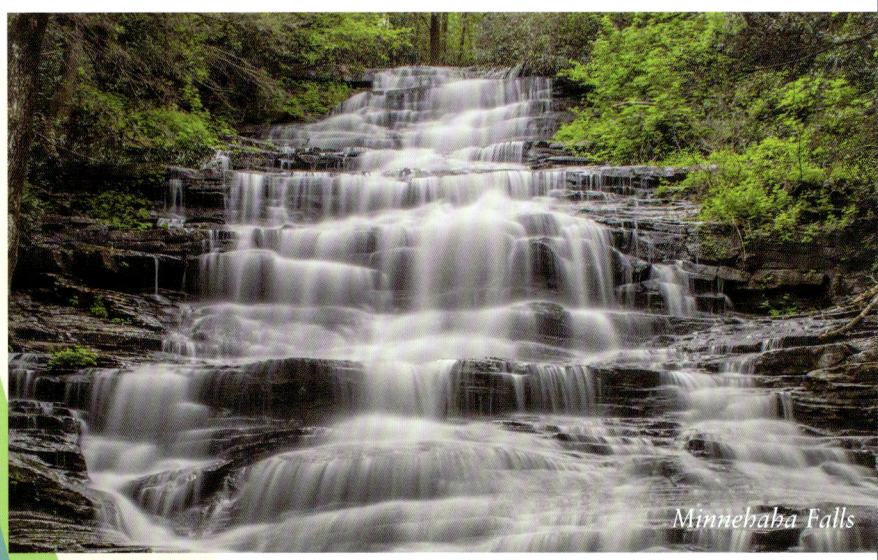

Minnehaha Falls

Below: Adairsville, Georgia town square

Peaches

Pecans

6

Okefenokee Swamp

ECOSYSTEM:

Georgia also offers a diverse ecosystem and is a nature lover's paradise. In the mountains, you may encounter white-tailed deer, black bears, barred owls, and skunks. Further south is where you can find the Okefenokee Swamp. Here you can kayak among alligators, turtles, and longnose gar. Head to the barrier islands off the Georgia coast to encounter loggerhead sea turtles, right whales, manatees, and wild horses on the beaches of Cumberland Island.

Atlanta in the early 1900s

Splashing fountains at Centennial Olympic Park.

Modern day Atlanta skyline

8

HISTORY OVERVIEW:

Georgia is rich in history dating back to 10,000 B.C.—a time when Native Americans called the land their home. The state is dotted with Indian mounds, rock effigies, and fortresses. You can visit these sacred places today and learn what it was like to live off the land as the Native Americans did.

Around 1540, the Europeans explored and settled what is known today as Georgia. Georgia was officially named and chartered by King George II in 1732. In 1776, Georgia was one of the 13 original colonies to sign the Declaration of Independence which formed the United States of America. There are many museums and parks which showcase this era in Georgia's history such as Fort King George, a rebuilt British fort from 1721.

Today, Atlanta is the capital of Georgia and is a magnet for businesses and industries. The state is a top location for the production of movies and television shows, and it has a vibrant music industry. It was also at the center of the American civil rights movement and became known as "the city too busy to hate."

Martin Luther King Jr. was a pastor at Ebenezer Baptist Church located in Atlanta until his death in 1968.

American Revolutionary War reenactment.

Nearly 4,000 of the 18,000 Cherokees who were forced to relocate died from disease, starvation, or exposure to the elements.

Chief Tomochichi

A Native American effigy created between 1000 B.C. and 1000 A.D. near Madison, Georgia called "Rock Eagle".

NATIVE AMERICAN HISTORY:

Before the Europeans arrived in North America, the land known today as Georgia was the home of Native Americans. They lived on the land since around 10,000 B.C., and the Cherokee made their capital in what is present-day Calhoun, GA. The Indian Removal Act led to their forceful relocation in the 1830s. The Native Americans left Georgia and relocated to reservations around what is present-day Oklahoma. Their long and arduous trek west became known as the Trail of Tears.

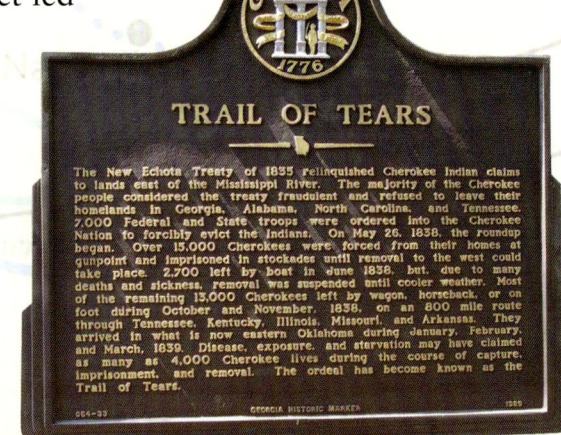

10

Left: Arrow heads used by Native Americans can be found near streams and rivers. Above: Home built in 1839 at McIntosh Reserve.

Chief William McIntosh was a prominent chief of the Creek Indian Nation.

Today, you can find Native American legacy all over the state by looking for arrow heads along the banks of streams and rivers or by visiting one of the many parks around the state such as McIntosh Reserve. Here, you can see a reconstructed log home from 1839, which is similar to that of Chief McIntosh's home.

You will notice many roads all over Atlanta are named "Peachtree". Many believe this actually has nothing to do with peaches. Atlanta was built on a Creek Indian Village and the Creeks called pine trees "pitch trees" due to their sap. Over time, "pitch tree" became peach tree!

Drawing of what villages looked like before being abandoned.

Indian mounds are scattered around the state.

LANDMARKS/POINTS OF INTEREST (POI):

Indian mounds dating back to 1000 A.D. can be found in several locations in Georgia including Cartersville, GA at the Etowah Indian Mounds and Blakely, GA at the Kolomoke Mounds State Park. The mounds were built to show status and serve as protection from invasions. The Chief lived on top of the tallest in each village.

At the Etowah Indian Mound site, there is a museum housing real Native American artifacts excavated from the site. There is an outdoor replica of a wattle and daub hut built the same way the Natives would have built them which you can go inside. You also can see how they dressed with shell beads, face paint, feathers, and copper ear ornaments. There are remnants of the v-shaped fish trap in the river, which Natives used to catch fish and tours where you can learn how they used trees for food and medicine.

TRIPP'S TIPS:
Search the banks of the Chattahoochee or Flint River for the best chance to find arrow heads!

Above: Stone Mountain. Right: Cable cars take you to the top of Stone Mountain.

You could call Stone Mountain the world's largest rock. It was created by a large magma chamber under the earth that cooled into rock. Thanks to millions of years of erosion, it has become known as the largest piece of exposed granite in the world. But what you see is just the very top of the mountain. It continues into the ground for another 9 miles!

You can walk 825 feet to the top which offers spectacular views of the Atlanta skyline and ride down the mountain in a Swiss cable car.

Firework display in front of Stone Mountain.

Civil War relief carved on the side of the mountain.

TRIPP'S TIPS:
Sit on Memorial Lawn when you visit Stone Mountain to watch the laser show cast on the side of the mountain while fireworks burst in the night sky!

Can you find a Confederate Yellow Daisy? The flower only grows around Stone Mountain. You can also spot small shrimp in the pools of water on top of the mountain! During long periods of drought, the eggs of these shrimp can lay dormant for years in the dry bowls. Once rain returns, the shrimp hatch again.

In Georgia, it's all about the peaches! The state is known as the Peach State because of its 130 million pounds of peaches grown each year. Georgia also produces more peanuts and pecans than any other state.

There are many orchards where you can go out into the fields and pick your own fruit or ride into the farm to see how these sweet fruits make it from the trees in Georgia to your kitchen table. Chances are there will be some homemade peach ice cream available to eat too!

Eating peaches picked right off a peach tree.

Lane Orchards located in Fort Valley, GA is a great place to get peaches and other fresh fruit.

Georgia's iconic red dirt roads are a common sight once you travel outside of the cities. The red clay was perfect for Native Americans to build wattle and daub huts in the state. Keep your eyes open because you don't want to miss your chance to buy some roadside food like watermelon, onions, peanuts, or pecans.

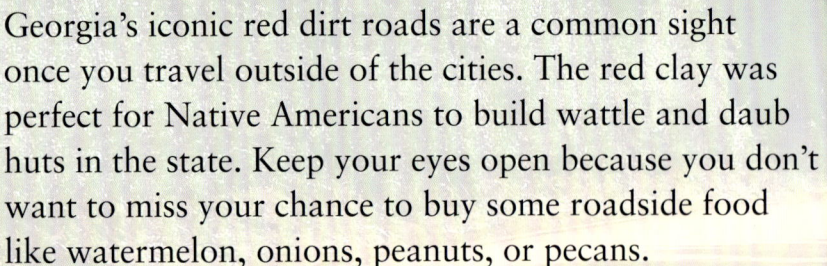
Wattle and daub hut at the Etowah Mounds in Cartersville, GA.

Homegrown fruits and vegetable stands are common in Georgia.

The Antebellum Inn Bed and Breakfast in Milledgeville, GA.

The Old Governor's Mansion in Milledgeville, GA completed in 1839.

You can walk through some of the largest, most extravagant homes built before 1860. They are known as antebellum homes. Georgia's mansions have been featured in numerous movies. You can even spend the night in some of the houses. Just follow the 100-mile long antebellum trail to see how the ultra-rich lived in the south, complete with period furniture and decorations.

TRIPP'S TIPS:
All along the antebellum trail, you will encounter historic covered bridges, governor's mansions, and perhaps even a Civil War reenactment. You can see what it was like on an 1850s cotton plantation and stand next to the giant columns of some of the most stately homes in the south.

17

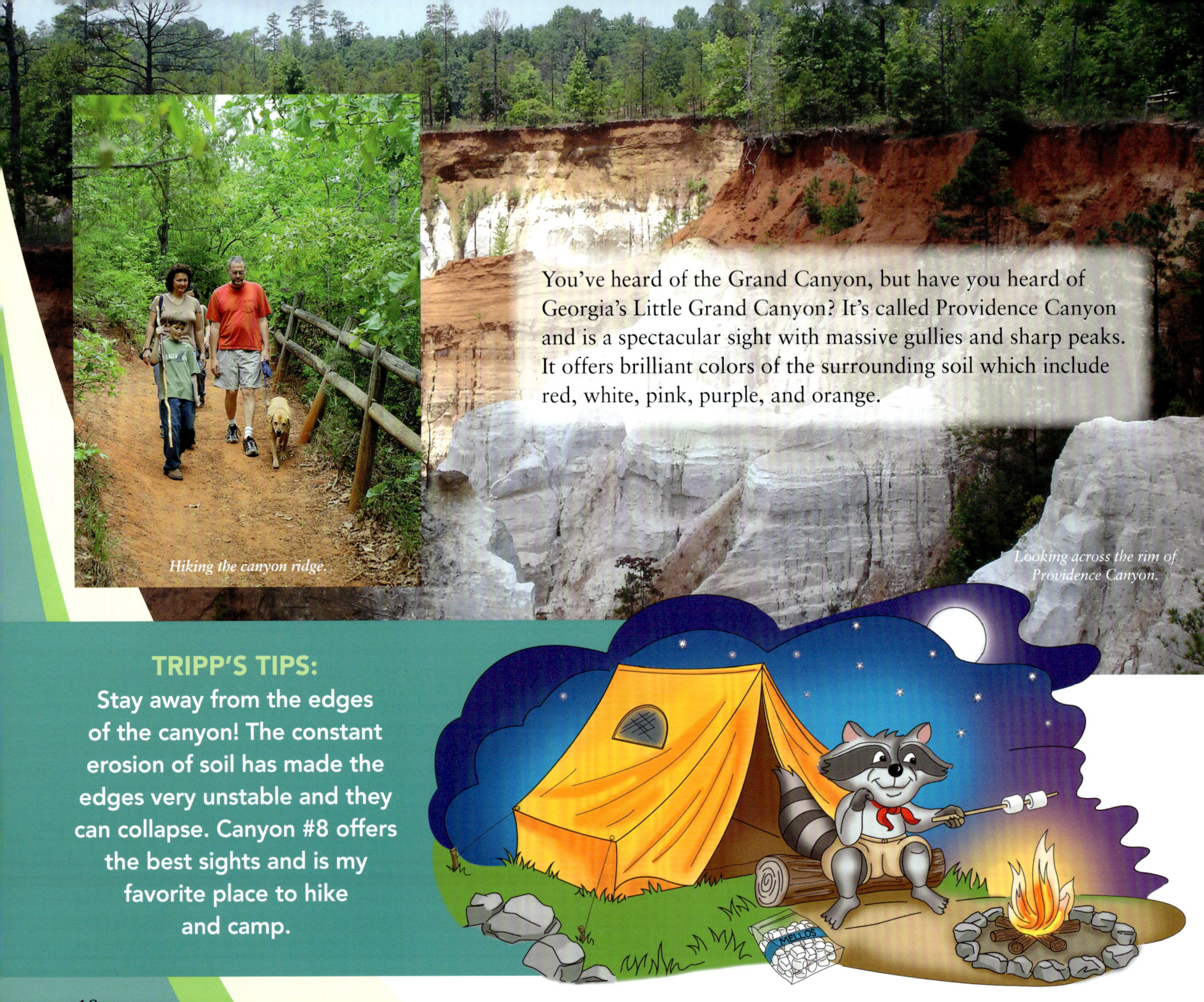

You've heard of the Grand Canyon, but have you heard of Georgia's Little Grand Canyon? It's called Providence Canyon and is a spectacular sight with massive gullies and sharp peaks. It offers brilliant colors of the surrounding soil which include red, white, pink, purple, and orange.

Hiking the canyon ridge.

Looking across the rim of Providence Canyon.

TRIPP'S TIPS:
Stay away from the edges of the canyon! The constant erosion of soil has made the edges very unstable and they can collapse. Canyon #8 offers the best sights and is my favorite place to hike and camp.

There are numerous trails and camp sites at Providence Canyon.

The canyon was created as a result of poor farming practices in the 1800s. Since the land had been stripped of native forest, small gullies rapidly grew deeper until they exposed soil that was deposited around 65 million years ago, right after the dinosaurs walked the Earth.

Providence Canyon is one of the most unusual geological formations in Georgia. There are 9 canyons to explore. Some of the deepest canyons can get very muddy (similar to quicksand) so wear your boots! It also is a camping destination and there are 10 miles of trails to hike.

Two whale sharks swim past onlookers.

Step into an underwater world at the largest aquarium in the United States. Georgia Aquarium lets you walk through a large acrylic tunnel surrounded by sharks, stingrays, sawfish, surgeonfish, and even whale sharks – the largest fish in the world.

Families and friends inside the acrylic tunnel viewing a variety of fish and sea creatures.

The Aquarium lets you see some of the most incredible animals in the world. See the weedy sea dragon or the Japanese spider crab in their icy cold habitats surrounded by kelp forests. You can also check out animals from freshwater climates, like the toothy piranha or the ever-popular river otters!

Encounter the sea otters.

Watch the jellies.

Peer at the weedy sea dragon.

Georgia Aquarium entrance.

Take a look at an African penguin.

21

TRIPP'S TIPS:
How would you like to sleep under the sea? After everyone else has left, you can sleep over at the Aquarium and watch your favorite fish all night!

Get close to a sea otter.

Interact with a dolphin.

Touch a penguin and see how their feathers feel.

23

Blackbeard Island

Many islands have both bay and ocean access within miles of each other.

Map of barrier islands.

GEORGIA ISLANDS:

The islands off the coast of Georgia are steeped in history and lore. Blackbeard Island is where Blackbeard the Pirate made his home and it is believed his loot and treasure are buried somewhere on the island. However, if you plan on going treasure hunting, the island is uninhabited and can only be accessed by boat, adding to the mystery surrounding the treasure.

Kayaking around an island.

Boating and fishing are popular along the coast.

Some islands are great vacation spots with biking, golfing, kayaking, sailing, and fishing. Other islands are protected seashores which are perfect for finding big sea shells, Loggerhead Sea Turtles, and other wildlife.

Wildlife is abundant near the Georgia coast.

Wild horses grazing in front of the ruins of Dungeness Mansion.

TRIPP'S TIPS:

Georgia's Cumberland Island is wild and untamed. You can only reach it by boat and it is almost completely undeveloped. There are wild horses running free on the beaches. Of the few structures on the island, the Carnegie mansions are a must see. The largest home, called Dungeness, is now in ruins and is slowly being reclaimed by the island.

For one of the most dramatic and coolest beaches in Georgia, head to Jekyll Island's Driftwood Beach. Driftwood Beach is like walking through a graveyard of petrified trees on a sandy beach. The result is a dramatic landscape where the skeletons of twisted trunks and branches stand their ground against the tides of the ocean. It's the perfect place to spend the day swimming in the ocean and taking incredible photographs.

Lounging in a hammock between tree trunks.

Driftwood Beach at sunset.

Tybee Island Lighthouse

When visiting the Georgia coast, be sure to climb the 178 stairs to the top of Tybee Island Lighthouse. The light station has been guiding ships into the Savannah River for over 285 years. If you're lucky, you may even spot some whales playing in the ocean.

Keith Jennings, creator of the "Tree Spirits of Saint Simon's Island".

TRIPP'S TIPS:
Keep a sharp eye out around St. Simon's Island and you may spot some of the island's tree spirits. These are carvings of faces made in the trunks of the oak trees that cover the island.

Exploring an underground gold mine.

THE FIRST GOLD RUSH:

Dahlonega, GA is a small, picturesque mountain town in the foothills of the Appalachian Mountains and is the site of one of America's first gold rushes. In fact, much of the outside dome of the capitol building in Atlanta is covered with gold mined from Dahlonega. There is still gold found by panning in mountain streams.

Left: Gold capitol building dome in Atlanta;
Top: Panning for gold and mine tours located at Consolidated Gold Mine in Dahlonega, GA.

TRIPP'S TIPS:

The best time to visit Helen is either in October when the town celebrates Oktoberfest or during Christkindlmarkt (Christmas Market) where the charm of Bavaria in the heart of Georgia really shines! There are concerts, German food and, of course, Santa and Mrs. Claus light up the town with Christmas lights!

The unique architecture in the town square of Helen, GA.

If you don't strike it rich in Dahlonega, head to Helen, GA which looks and feels like a Bavarian mountain town complete with mountain streams you can float down, pointed red roofed buildings, and numerous waterfalls. In 1968, local businessmen discussed how they could make Helen stand out from the rest of the cities. They met with an artist who had been stationed in Germany and they decided to begin decorating the buildings and roads to mimic an Alpine village. You will think you are in Germany!

Floating down the Chattahoochee River in Helen, GA.

River Street in Savannah.

Wherever you are from, Savannah will welcome you with true southern hospitality. Here, history is quite literally beneath your feet.

Be sure to eat plenty of homemade fudge and candy on the historic cobblestone road of River Street. The stones were originally used in ships as a ballast and unloaded when they reached the Savannah harbor. Settlers of Savannah then used the stones to build their roads.

Historic buildings, shops, and restaurants along the cobblestone roads on River Street beside Savannah River.

31

Riverboat in Savannah, GA.

As you walk away from the river and into the city, you will enter an area where the sun struggles to reach the ground through the Spanish moss and huge limbs of the oak trees which dominate the sky. Here you will encounter the many statues, fountains, and monuments which adorn the 22 famous squares of Savannah. Forsyth Fountain in Savannah is one of the most photographed and painted spots in Georgia!

Forsyth Fountain in Savannah, GA.

TRIPP'S TIPS:

Juliette Gordon Low, the founder of Girl Scouts of the USA, was born in Savannah. You can take a ride on a river ferry which bears her name and travels up and down the Savannah River. You can also tour her childhood home located on Oglethorpe Avenue.

32

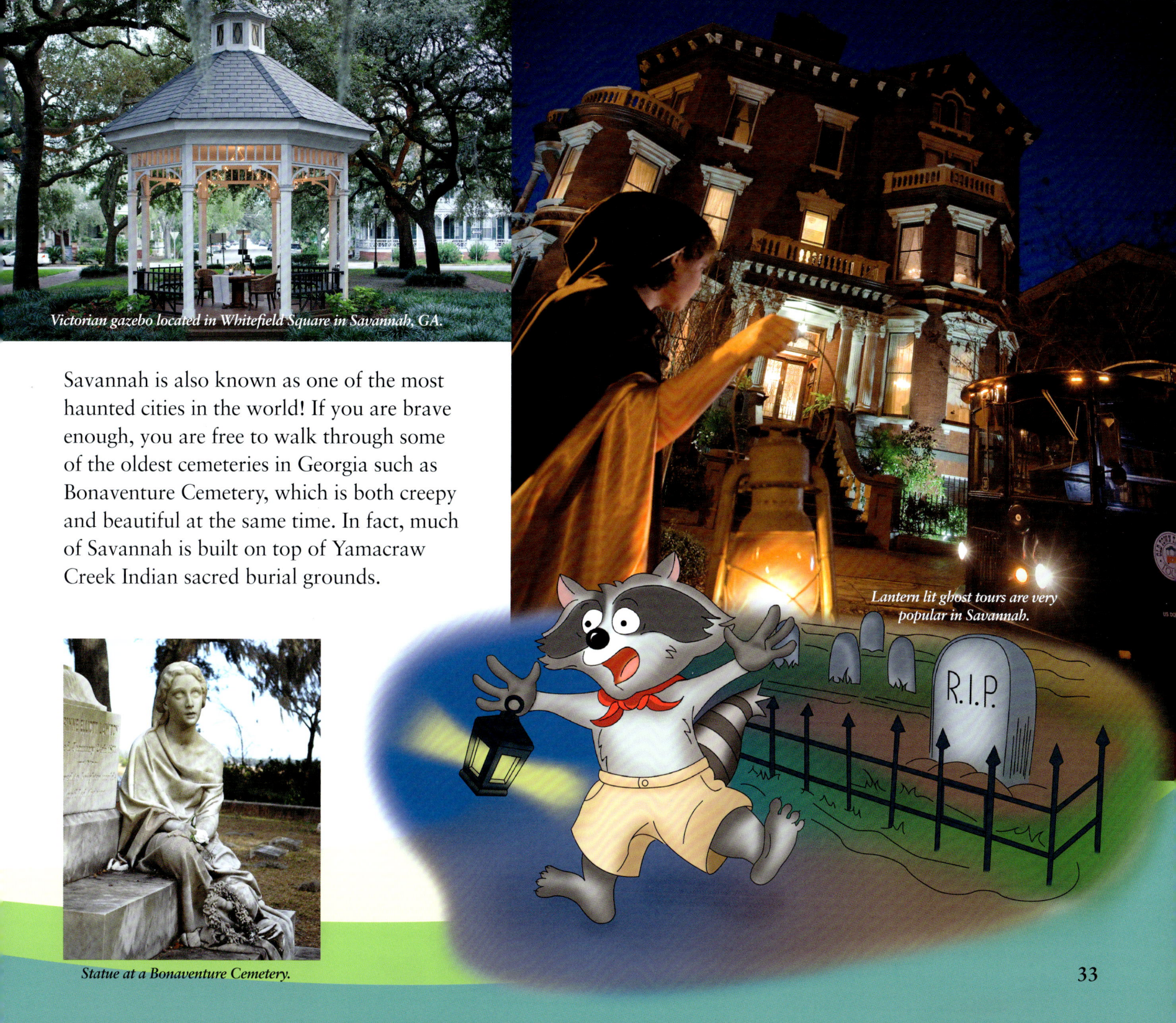

Victorian gazebo located in Whitefield Square in Savannah, GA.

Savannah is also known as one of the most haunted cities in the world! If you are brave enough, you are free to walk through some of the oldest cemeteries in Georgia such as Bonaventure Cemetery, which is both creepy and beautiful at the same time. In fact, much of Savannah is built on top of Yamacraw Creek Indian sacred burial grounds.

Lantern lit ghost tours are very popular in Savannah.

Statue at a Bonaventure Cemetery.

Wormsloe Historic Site entrance and tree tunnel.

Wormsloe Historic Site showcases the oldest standing structure in Savannah and one of the most picturesque places in Georgia. The entrance boasts a mile-long tunnel of trees created by huge live oaks. You also may encounter employees in period costumes demonstrating what it was like to live on the site.

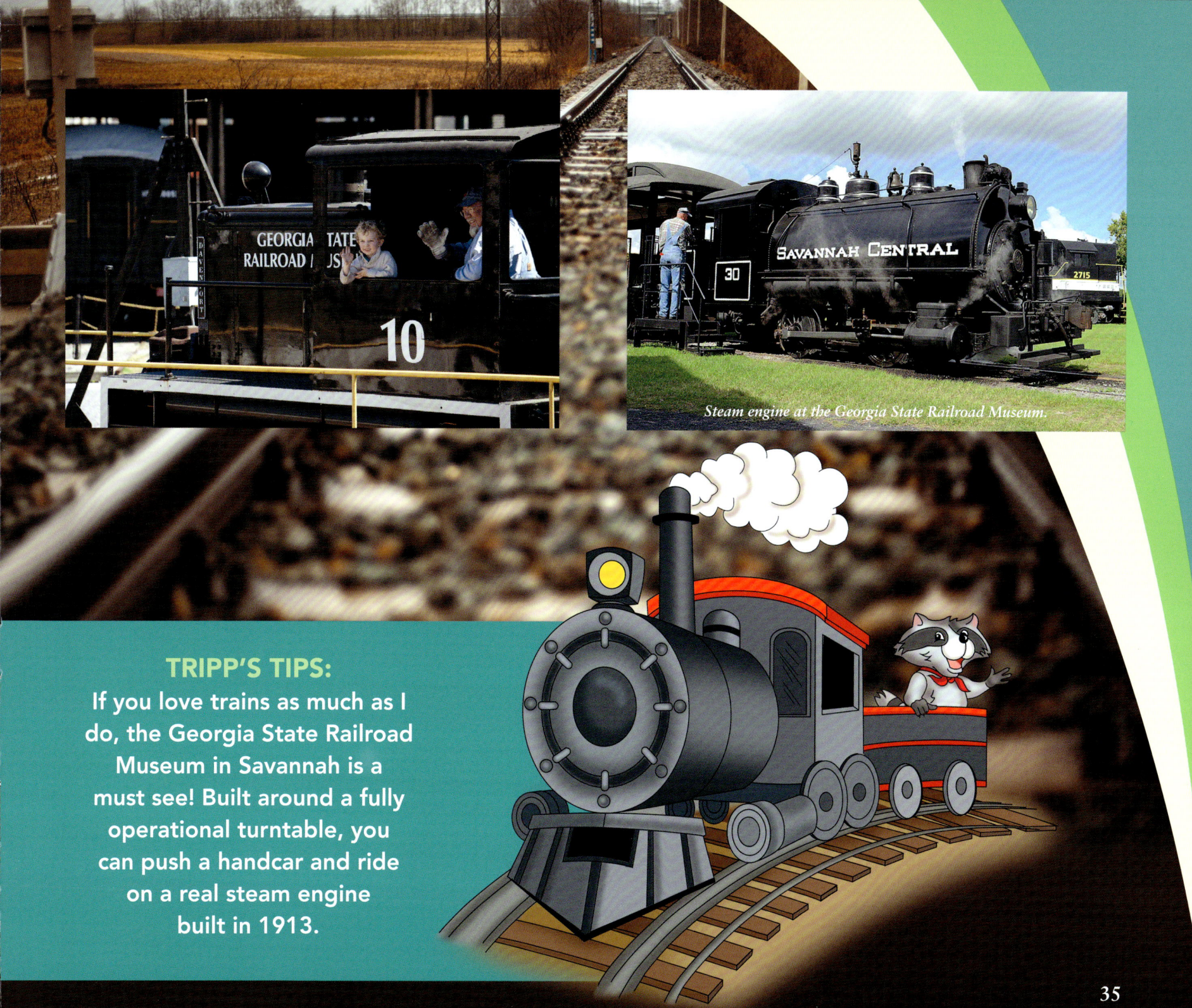

Steam engine at the Georgia State Railroad Museum.

TRIPP'S TIPS:
If you love trains as much as I do, the Georgia State Railroad Museum in Savannah is a must see! Built around a fully operational turntable, you can push a handcar and ride on a real steam engine built in 1913.

Tallulah Gorge

Amicalola Falls

Minnehaha Falls

Anna Ruby Falls

TRIPP'S TIPS:
Don't forget to visit some of Georgia's waterfalls. One of my favorite falls is Amicalola Falls. It is 729 feet tall and the tallest waterfall in the state. Other spectacular waterfalls are Anna Ruby Falls near Helen, the stair stepping falls of Minnehaha, and the can't-miss Tallulah Falls at Tallulah Gorge State Park. Here you can view the falls on a swaying bridge suspended 80-feet in the air.

One of the many scenic views along the Appalachian Trail.

Path along the Appalachian Trail.

When you are done exploring Georgia and ready to go to your next adventure, don't drive or fly. Hike the Appalachian Trail. The trail begins at Springer Mountain in Ellijay, Georgia and ends in Katahdin, Maine. Only 1 in 4 people who try to hike the entire 2,190-mile trail are able to finish. It can take up to 7 months of nonstop walking to complete. But, you don't have to hike all the way to Maine because there are plenty of trails that can be hiked as day trips that have beautiful views of the mountains.

GLOSSARY:

accessed (AK-ses) Capable of being reached; to enter.

acrylic (uh-KRIL-ik) A type of hard, clear plastic.

adorn (uh-DAWRN) To add beauty to; decorate.

antebellum (an-tee-BEL-uhm) The period of time before the American Civil War.

arduous (AHR-joo-uhs) A journey with great difficulty, exertion, or endurance.

artifacts (AHR-tuh-fakts) Objects made by human beings.

barrier island (BAR-ee-er) Long, narrow islands which protect the mainland from storms.

centennial (sen-TEN-ee-uhl) 100 years.

chartered (CHAHR-ter) An official document given by a government or ruler to a business or other group. The charter explains the group's rights and responsibilities.

confederate (kuhn-FED-er-it) The southern United States during the Civil War, which were confederates in their fight to secede from the rest of the country.

diverse (dih-VURS) Made up of different things.

dormant (DAWR-muhnt) Not active; at rest.

drought (DROUT) A long period of time without rain.

effigy (EF-i-jee) An image or representation.

excavated (EKS-kuh-veyt) To uncover by digging.

expansive (ik-SPAN-siv) Large; magnificent.

extravagant (ik-STRAV-uh-guhnt) Expensive, excessive, or over the top.

gazebo (guh-ZEE-boh) A small roofed building affording shade and rest.

gullies (GUHL-ee) A deep ditch cut by running water.

hospitality (hos-pi-TAL-i-tee) The friendly, warm, and generous treatment of guests or strangers.

immerse (ih-MURS) To involve deeply; devote oneself fully.

laser (LAY-zer) A device that produces an intense beam of light.

legacy (LEG-uh-see) Something handed down from one generation to the next.

lore (LOHR) A body of knowledge or tradition that is passed down among members of a culture.

magma (MAG-muh) Hot, liquid matter beneath the earth's surface that cools to form igneous rock.

memorial (muh-MAWR-ee-uhl) Anything that symbolizes or celebrates someone who died.

picturesque (PIK-chuh-resk) Something that is pleasing or interesting to look at.

reenactment (re-en-AKT-muhnt) The recreation of an event.

reservations (rez-er-VAY-shuhn) An area of land set aside by the U.S. Government for the use of Native Americans.

remnants (REM-nuhnt) Remaining traces of something.

replica (REP-li-kuh) A duplication or copy.

spectacular (spek-TAK-yuh-ler) Causing feelings of wonder; excellent or amazing.

status (STAT-uhs) A person's rank in a group.

uninhabited (un-in-HAB-i-tid) An area of land where people do not live.

unique (yoo-NEEK) Being the only one of its type or kind.

wattle and daub hut (WAT-l and DAWB huht) A framework of woven rods and twigs, covered and plastered with clay and used in building construction.

PHOTO CREDITS:

Cover front top right: ©Georgia Aquarium; top inset: George Hodan/PublicDomainPictures.net; middle & bottom inset: Georgia State Parks & Historic Sites. Back cover left to right: Christian Murillo/Murillo Photography, @cmurillophoto; ExploreGeorgia.org; National Park Service; Meitra Lak Perry

Page 6 top right: Sean Pavone /Adobe Photo Stock; left middle: ©Erinkate25/Dreamstime.com; center inset: ExploreGeorgia.org; left inset: National Park Service Gallery; right inset: ExploreGeorgia.org; bottom right: ©2019 Shutterstock

Page 7 Georgia State Parks & Historic Sites; inset: Christian Murillo/Murillo Photography, @cmurillophoto

Page 8 right: Pixabay.com; top inset: Library of Congress; bottom inset: ExploreGeorgia.org

Page 9 top: Library of Congress; bottom: Georgia State Parks & Historic Sites

Page 10 right: National Library of Medicine; top inset: Wikipedia.org; bottom left inset: ExploreGeorgia.org; bottom right inset: ©David Seibert

Page 11 top left: Meitra Lak Perry; right: robin/yelp; right inset: Charles Bird King/Smithsonian.edu; center inset: ExploreGeorgia.org

Page 12 left: HR/Wikipedia.org; right: Georgia State Parks & Historic Sites

Page 13 top: G Allen Penton/©2019 Shutterstock.com; inset: Pixabay.com

Page 14 left: kurdistan/©2019 Shutterstock.com; inset: pilotguy/Wikipedia.org; top inset: Alan Cressler/Wildfbottom Center Digital Library

Page 15 top: Dreamtime.com; bottom: National Park Service Gallery; background ExploreGeorgia.org

Page 16 left: 123RF.com; top: Meitra Lak Perry; bottom: ExploreGeorgia.org

Page 17 ExploreGeorgia.org; antebellumtrail.org

Page 18 left inset: Georgia State Parks & Historic Sites; right: ExporeGeorgia.org

Page 19 left & top right: Georgia State Parks & Historic Sites; middle inset: ExploreGeorgia.org; bottom right: ©2019 Shutterstock.com

Page 20–23: ©Georgia Aquarium

Page 24 left: U.S. Fish & Wildlife Service; right: Courtesy of Seal Island

Page 25 top left, top right & middle right: Georgia State Parks & Historic Sites top left inset: U.S. Fish & Wildlife Service; middle left inset: Kirk Rogers/USFWS National Digital Library; bottom left inset: Pixabay.com

Page 26 National Park Service

Page 27 inset right & left: Christian Murillo/Murillo Photography, @cmurillophoto; background photo, ©2019 Shutterstock

Page 28 left: ExploreGeorgia.org; right & inset: Courtesy of Keith Jennings

Page 29 Georgia State Parks & Historic Sites; top: ExploreGeorgia.org

Page 30 top: Pixabay.com; bottom: marvelmurugan.com

Page 31 top: ©Sean Pavone/Dreamstime.com; bottom Wikipedia; middle & bottom insets: ExploreGeorgia.org; bottom 123RF.com

Page 32 left: © Sean Pavone/Shutterstock.com; pixabay.com; right: Dreamsline.com

Page 33 ExploreGeorgia.org; inset: Pixabay.com

Page 34 Georgia State Parks & Historic Sites

Page 35 left inset: ExploreGeorgia.org; right inset: Nikonites.com; background: SpiltShire/Pexels.com

Page 36 left: ©Erinkate25/Dreamstime.com; right: Ancha Chiangmai/©2019 Shutterstock.com; top inset: Georgia State Parks & Historic Sites; bottom inset: Pixabay.com

Page 37 inset: Christian Murillo/Murillo Photography, @cmurillophoto; background: ExploreGeorgia.org

SPECIAL THANKS TO:

Lisa Greenleaf Design Studio
www.lisagreenleaf.com
Lisa@Lisagreenleaf.com

Christian Murillo Photography, LLC
www.murillophoto.com
786-390-1035

Stone Mountain Park
1000 Robert E. Lee Blvd
Stone Mountain, GA 30083
www.stonemountainpark.com
1-800-401-2407

Georgia Aquarium
225 Baker St NW
Atlanta, GA 30313
www.georgiaaquarium.org
404-581-4000

Georgia State Railroad Museum
655 Louisville Road
Savannah, GA 31401
www.chsgeorgia.org/GSRM
912-651-6840

Georgia State Parks
2600 Highway 155 SW
Stockbridge, GA 30281
www.gastateparks.org
1-800-864-7275

Lane Orchards
50 Lane Road
Fort Valley, GA 31030
www.lanesouthernorchards.com

ABOUT THE AUTHORS:

Meitra Lak Perry currently works as a high school counselor where she has been named Counselor of the Year in her school district, featured in industry journals, and was a recipient of the 30 under 30 award by the University of West Georgia. She currently holds an Education Specialist degree in School Counseling while working on her Doctorate of Education in Counseling and Supervision. Meitra's passion is helping high school students from underrepresented populations reach their highest potential.

Michael Perry is an avid outdoorsman who gained a passion for nature and traveling while earning his rank as an Eagle Scout. Even after several stints abroad, traveling and being immersed in other cultures still inspires him the most, both professionally and personally.

Michael and Meitra met while attending the University of West Georgia and married in 2014. They continue to live in the West Georgia region with their two daughters, Abigail and Elizabeth.

ABOUT THE ILLUSTRATOR:

Lisa Greenleaf is a New Hampshire award-winning illustrator, author and book designer. Her images and stories have graced many children's books including, *John Greenleaf Whittier's The Barefoot Boy*, *Feathers & Trumpets A Story of Hildegard of Bingen*, *When Rivers Burned: The Earth Day Story*, and the *America's Notable Women Series*.

Lisa continues to follow her passion for art and design and has a successful design business, *Greenleaf Design Studio*. She has been featured in the news, TV, radio, art shows and book events. Lisa is an accomplished motivational speaker and has made many presentations at events and programs, sharing her stories, anecdotes, inspirational messages, music, and tools that she incorporates throughout her work and daily life.

When Lisa takes a little break from her artsy side, you can find her exploring with her two millenial kids or kayaking along the NH and MA rivers and shores. In the evenings, she is frequently singing and playing her ukulele at open mic venues or performing at gigs with her husband, Bob Pope. www.LisaGreenleaf.com